GETTING TO KNOW
THE U.S. PRESIDENTS

ULYSSES S.
GRANT

EIGHTEENTH PRESIDENT
1869 – 1877

WRITTEN AND ILLUSTRATED BY MIKE VENEZIA

CHILDREN'S PRESS®
A DIVISION OF SCHOLASTIC INC.
NEW YORK   TORONTO   LONDON   AUCKLAND   SYDNEY
MEXICO CITY   NEW DELHI   HONG KONG
DANBURY, CONNECTICUT

Reading Consultant: Nanci R. Vargus, Ed.D., Assistant Professor, School of Education, University of Indianapolis

Historical Consultant: Marc J. Selverstone, Ph.D., Assistant Professor, Miller Center of Public Affairs, University of Virginia

Photographs © 2005: Art Resource, NY: 12 top (National Portrait Gallery, Smithsonian Institution, Washington DC, U.S.A.), 28 (Scala); Corbis Images: 27 (Bettmann), 21 (PoodlesRock), 25; Courtesy of Galena/Jo Daviess County Historical Society & Museum: 16; Getty Images: 26 (Michael Smith), 29 (Hulton Archive); Library of Congress: 32 (via Soda), 12 bottom, 20, 22, 24; Ohio Historical Society/Ulysses S. Grant Presidential Collection: 6 right; Robertstock.com: 23; Stock Montage, Inc.: 6 left, 13; White House Historical Association: 3.

Colorist for illustrations: Dave Ludwig

Library of Congress Cataloging-in-Publication Data

Venezia, Mike.
  Ulysses S. Grant / written and illustrated by Mike Venezia.
    p. cm. – (Getting to know the U.S. presidents)
  ISBN 0-516-22623-1 (lib. bdg.)   0-516-25488-X (pbk.)
1. Grant, Ulysses S. (Ulysses Simpson), 1822-1885—Juvenile
literature. 2. Presidents—United States—Biography—Juvenile
literature. 3. Generals—United States—-Biography—Juvenile
literature. 4. United States. Army—Biography—-Juvenile literature.
I. Title.
  E672.V46 2005
  973.8'2'092–dc22

                                                    2004022572

1 2 3 4 5 6 7 8 9 10 R 14 13 12 11 10 09 08 07 06 05

A portrait
of President
Ulysses S. Grant

Ulysses S. Grant was born in 1822 in Point Pleasant, Ohio. He became the eighteenth president of the United States in 1869. Ulysses was elected president because he was a great Civil War general. Unfortunately, people later realized that being a war hero didn't necessarily make a person a good president.

Ulysses S. Grant was a general in the Union army. He won battle after battle against the southern Confederate army. Ulysses was known for making good decisions and acting quickly to carry them out. When he became president, though, Ulysses found he wasn't dealing with disciplined soldiers anymore.

President Grant now had to work with lots of different people who were trying to get things done their way. Ulysses S. Grant wasn't used to making compromises. He also didn't have the experience to deal with skilled politicians.

Grant's boyhood home in Georgetown, Ohio

Ulysses S. Grant's parents, Hannah and Jesse Grant

When Ulysses was a boy growing up in Ohio, his parents noticed that he had a remarkable talent. He got along with horses better than anyone. When he was very young, Ulysses would often play underneath teams of horses that were hitched up in front of his father's business.

Ulysses would even swing back and forth on the horses' tails. People passing by would panic and run to tell Ulysses' parents that their son was in danger. Mrs. Grant always said she wasn't worried. Ulysses seemed to understand horses and they seemed to understand him.

Ulysses S. Grant's father owned a tannery. A tannery is a factory in which animal skins are processed and made into leather. Ulysses hated the tannery, though. He told his father he would rather do anything than work around vats of smelly chemicals, bones, and animal skins. Ulysses couldn't stand the sight of blood, either. Mr. Grant did what he could to give his son jobs to do outside the tannery.

9

Ulysses was just an average student in grade school. When it came time for him to go to college, Ulysses' father arranged for him to go to the United States Military Academy at West Point, New York. Ulysses was shocked. He was afraid he would flunk out, and he didn't want to disappoint anyone. He followed his father's wishes, though, and left for the academy in 1839.

Ulysses was just an average student at West Point, too, but he was able to show off his skill at horsemanship. He set a record jump on horseback there that lasted twenty-five years!

Students at West Point are expected to serve in the army after they graduate. When Ulysses graduated, he hoped to get into the cavalry, the horseback division of the army. But because of his low grades and some discipline problems, he was assigned to the infantry. Infantry soldiers fight on foot.

Grant served as an officer (left) during the Mexican War (below).

In 1843, Ulysses S. Grant became a supply officer in the U.S. Army. He was sent to a post near St. Louis, Missouri. He met a girl there and fell deeply in love with her. Julia Dent came from a wealthy farming family. Ulysses and Julia got engaged. A few years later, Ulysses went off to serve in the Mexican War.

A portrait of Julia Dent Grant

The United States' war with Mexico lasted from 1846 to 1848. Ulysses S. Grant learned many things during the war that would help him years later. He served under two of the best generals in the United States, Zachary Taylor and Winfield Scott. Because he had been a supply officer, Ulysses understood exactly what kinds of food and equipment soldiers needed while fighting battles.

Unfortunately, during the war, Ulysses picked up some bad habits that would later ruin his health. He began smoking cigars and drinking lots of whiskey.

After the United States won the Mexican War, Ulysses returned to St. Louis and married Julia. Ulysses served in the army for another six years. He and Julia began raising a family. Ulysses kept getting transferred from one lonely army outpost to another. A homesick Ulysses began drinking more and becoming quarrelsome. In 1854, he was asked to resign from the army. Ulysses was very glad to return to Julia and his children.

Ulysses first tried to make a living by farming, but failed when his crops fizzled out. Next he tried a real-estate job, but that didn't work out either. Finally, even though he hated to do it, Ulysses asked his father for help. Mr. Grant gave his son a job as a clerk in one of the family's leather-goods stores.

Galena as it looked in the 1850s

Ulysses went to work for his younger brother in Galena, Illinois. He did his job quietly, selling leather goods and spending lots of time with his family. Hardly anyone in Galena noticed him, but that would soon change.

About a year after Ulysses started his new job, the Civil War began. For years, people in the United States had been arguing over the issue of slavery. In 1861, the southern states finally decided to leave the United States and form their own country, the Confederate States of America. People in the North didn't believe the South had any right to form their own country. This disagreement soon led to America's bloodiest war ever. Ulysses S. Grant offered to help the northern army by training men to fight.

Since Ulysses was one of the few men around with military experience, he was immediately given the job of training volunteers. People said that the volunteers in his area were some of the nastiest, laziest, untrainable men around. Ulysses never gave up, though, and finally turned them into a group of excellent soldiers.

Right away, Ulysses and his volunteers won some battles against Confederate troops. Because of this success, Ulysses was promoted to brigadier general. General Grant then won two important bigger battles that took place in Tennessee. Newspapers began reporting stories about his victories. Almost overnight, General Ulysses S. Grant became a national hero. He also became President Lincoln's favorite general.

An illustration showing Grant and his generals during the Civil War

President Lincoln had trouble with his generals at the beginning of the Civil War. At times, they hesitated to send their men into battle. They also couldn't decide how to fight the Confederate army. Ulysses S. Grant seemed to be the only general who was willing to fight, and when he fought, he usually won.

This postcard shows President Lincoln meeting with General Grant.

Meeting of President LINCOLN and Gen'l GRANT.

General Grant was always calm, no matter how many shells were exploding around him or bullets were flying by. He gave orders confidently. His confidence gave his men hope, even in the worst of times. In 1862, President Lincoln showed his appreciation by promoting Ulysses S. Grant to major general.

Richmond, Virginia, was among the southern cities that were destroyed during the Civil War.

General Grant won victory after victory. Often, thousands of lives were lost on both sides during these battles. Sometimes General Grant was criticized for being too brutal, but he believed brutal force was the only way to end the war. Finally, Grant's army trapped the Confederate army near their capital city, Richmond, Virginia.

At a small village near Richmond called Appomattox, the great southern general Robert E. Lee surrendered to General Grant. On April 9, 1865, after four years of horrible war, the fighting ended. General Grant showed surprising respect for General Lee and his army by letting them keep their sidearms and horses.

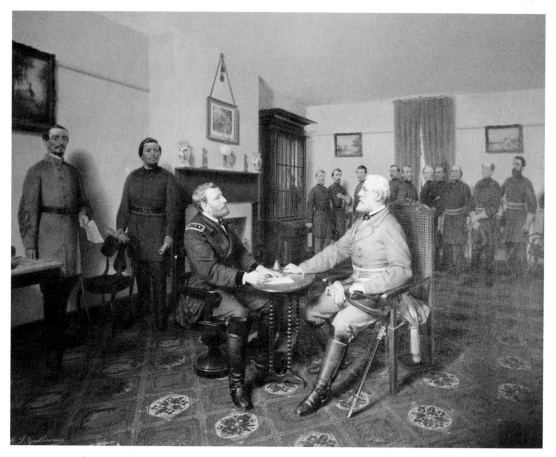

A painting showing Robert E. Lee (right) surrendering to Ulysses S. Grant (left)

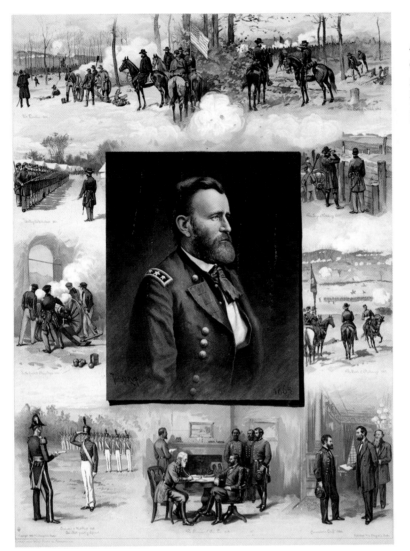

A heroic portrait of General Grant surrounded by famous scenes from his military career

President Lincoln showed his appreciation once more by making Ulysses S. Grant general of all U.S. armies. No one had been given that rank since George Washington! In less than four years, Ulysses S. Grant had gone from pretty much being a failure to the most popular military hero in the United States.

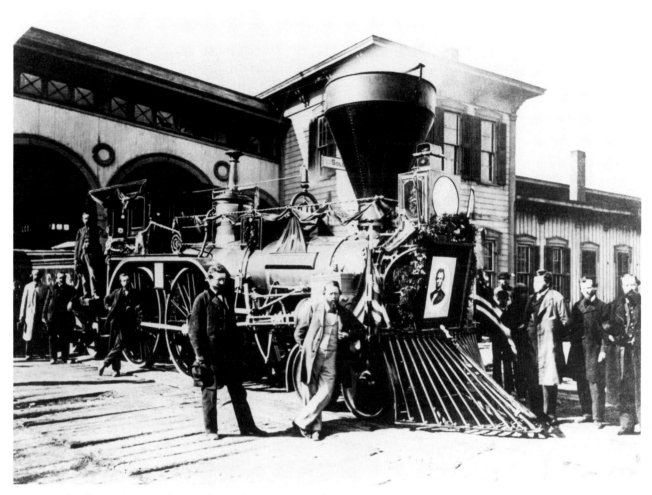

The funeral train of President Abraham Lincoln

Tragically, only five days after the Civil War ended, President Lincoln was assassinated. Vice President Andrew Johnson took over right away. Unfortunately, he didn't do a very good job. By the time President Johnson's term was ending, people were excited about nominating their favorite Civil War hero as the next president.

Ulysses S. Grant was inaugurated president on March 4, 1869.

Ulysses S. Grant won the presidential election of 1868. His biggest challenge now was how to get the defeated southern states back on their feet and into the Union again. Reconstruction was the name of the plan to rebuild southern towns and cities. President Johnson hadn't been able to get much done for Reconstruction.

Reconstruction included finding homes for and protecting the rights of 4 million former slaves. President Grant worked hard to protect the former slaves. He made sure the Fifteenth Amendment was added to the Constitution. This amendment guaranteed the right to vote no matter what race or color a man was.

The end of the Civil War brought slaves their freedom, but most slaves were left without a place to live.

Across the Continent, Westward the Course of Empire Takes Its Way,
by Currier & Ives (Museum of the City of New York)

President Grant was popular enough to be elected for a second four-year term. Many exciting things were going on in the United States during this time. Railroads connected the country from coast to coast. More land was being settled in the West and new towns and cities were popping up all over.

People from foreign nations poured into the country to help build cities and work in factories. Unfortunately, American Indians suffered badly during this time. The American government forced them off land that was rightly theirs. President Grant set up a commission to deal with the Indian situation.

In 1876, in an effort to force Indians off lands in Montana, U.S. troops attacked Cheyenne and Sioux Indians in what became known as the Battle of the Little Bighorn.

Ulysses S. Grant's biggest mistake as president was choosing old friends to help him run the country. Most of these friends had very little political experience. Many of them began behaving badly, too, by accepting bribes and stealing money from taxes.

President Grant trusted his advisors and often found out about their cheating and crooked dealings after it was too late. Even though President Grant was always honest himself, these disgraceful activities hurt his reputation.

A photograph of Grant writing his autobiography during his last days

In 1876, just before President Grant left office, he made a remarkable speech. He apologized for making mistakes and showing poor judgment.

Over the next few years, bad investments left Ulysses S. Grant almost broke. Shortly before he died on July 23, 1885, he wrote a book about his life. *Personal Memoirs of U.S. Grant* was so successful that it allowed his family to live comfortably for the rest of their lives.